Dear Parent:

Your child's love of reading starts here!

Every child learns to read in a different way and at his or her own
speed. Some go back and forth between
favorite books again and again. Oth
order. You can help your young rea
confident by encouraging his or her
books your child reads with you to
alone, there are I Can Read Books fo. every stage of reading:

SHARED READING
Basic language, word repetition, and whimsical illustrations,
ideal for sharing with your emergent reader

BEGINNING READING
Short sentences, familiar words, and simple concepts
for children eager to read on their own

READING WITH HELP
Engaging stories, longer sentences, and language play
for developing readers

READING ALONE
Complex plots, challenging vocabulary, and high-interest topics
for the independent reader

I Can Read Books have introduced children to the joy of reading
since 1957. Featuring award-winning authors and illustrators and a
fabulous cast of beloved characters, I Can Read Books set the
standard for beginning readers.

A lifetime of discovery begins with the magical words "I Can Read!"

*Visit www.icanread.com for information
on enriching your child's reading experience.*

**Visit www.zonderkidz.com/icanread for more faith-based
I Can Read! titles from Zonderkidz.**

"Be strong and brave. Do not be terrified. Do not lose hope. I am the Lord your God. I will be with you everywhere you go."
— *Joshua 1:9* NIrV

ZONDERKIDZ

Joshua Crosses the Jordan River
Copyright © 2011 by Zondervan
Illustrations © 2011 by Valerie Sokolova

An **I Can Read Book**

Requests for information should be addressed to:
Zonderkidz, 3900 *Sparks Drive SE, Grand Rapids, Michigan 49546*

Library of Congress Cataloging-in-Publication Data

Bowman, Crystal.
    Joshua crosses the Jordan River / by Crystal Bowman.
        p. cm. — (I can read levels. Level one)
    Illustrated by Valerie Sokolova.
    ISBN 978-0-310-72156-7 (softcover)
    1. Joshua (Biblical figure)—Juvenile literature. 2. Bible stories, English—O.T. Joshua. 3. Jordan
    River—Juvenile literature. I. Sokolova, Valerie. II. Title.
    BS580.J7B68 2011
    222'.20950—dc2   201001653

Editor: Mary Hassinger
Art direction: Jody Langley

Printed in China
20 /SCC/ 10 9 8 7 6 5

Joshua Crosses the Jordan

Story by Crystal Bowman
Pictures by Valerie Sokolova

Moses was the leader

of God's people.

He helped God's people

cross through the Red Sea.

They were no longer

slaves in Egypt.

Moses grew to be very old,

and then he died.

The people were sad.

But God did not want

his people to be sad.

He gave them a new leader.

His name was Joshua.

God said to Joshua,

"You must lead my people

into a new land."

It was a land with rivers and trees
and lots of good food to eat.

Joshua wanted to help God's people

get to their new land.

But first they had to cross

a big river.

It was called the Jordan River.

"Be strong and brave," God said

to Joshua.

"Do not be afraid.

I will be with you."

Joshua told all the people
to get ready.
"In three days we will cross
the Jordan River," he said.
"Then God will give us
our new land."

So all the people got ready

to move to the new land.

They packed up all their things

and camped by the Jordan River.

The river was very deep and wide.

The people wondered how they could

all get across the big river.

But Joshua was not afraid.

He knew that God

would be with them.

God said to Joshua,

"Walk to the banks

of the Jordan River.

Tell the priests to step

into the river.

Then they must stop."

Joshua led the people to the river.

The priests stepped into the river,

and then they stopped.

Then God did a great thing!

He made the river stop flowing.

Soon the water was gone

and the ground was dry.

All the people walked

on dry ground to the other side.

Moms and dads,

brothers and sisters,

grandpas and grandmas

all crossed the Jordan River.

Then God said to Joshua,

"Pick twelve men.

Tell each of them to take a stone

from the middle of the river.

Then put the stones in a pile

where you stay tonight."

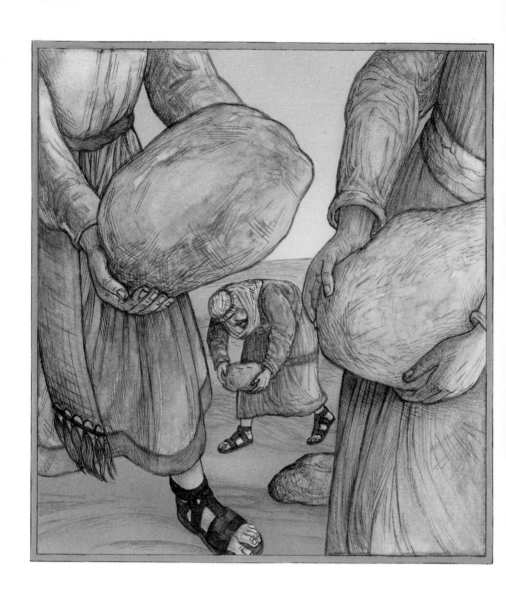

Joshua picked twelve men.

They each took a stone

from the middle of the river.

Then they put the stones in a pile

just like God told them to do.

God said to Joshua,

"Someday your children will ask you

about these stones.

Then you can tell them
how you crossed the Jordan River
on dry ground."

Soon the water started to flow.

The river was deep and wide again.

But the twelve special stones

would help the people to remember

what God did for them that day.